Not
Wholesome
Content

Samantha EJ Button

For the Three Musketeers

Never on plan
Always a smile
Often a lesson
Makes life worthwhile

Contents

Blood & Love

For Marples	1
Activist	2
In Your Eyes	4
The Girl With The Red Hair	6
Claire	8
Clara	10
All The Players; All The Daggers	12
Befall	16
Rose Tinted Spectacles	17
Narcissist	18
You Bet	22
The Carer	24
Investigators	26
Conditioning	28
Black Cat	30
Spoils	31
Yet	32

Fear & Rage

Every Hour	34
She	36
Revenge	38
Anxiety	39
The Ballerina	40
Why	42
Sweetheart	44
Her Tongue Was A Weapon	45
The Stamp Collector	46
Merry-Go-Round	48
Hey	50
What Happened To You?	52
Karma	54
How Much?	56

Gratitude

Perfectly Perfect   59
Face Off   60
I Have Time to Learn   62
Shotguns   63
Review   64
Nina   66
Shiny Floor   68
Box of Treasure   69
Gratitude   70
The Lady in the Post Office   72
Say it Now   74
The Queue   75
Those Who Know, Know   76

Authors Note

Please be aware that this book contains reference to issues that some readers may find distressing. These include:

Narcissism and gaslighting
Sexual assault
Femicide
Violence
Bereavement and loss
Speciesism
Chronic and serious illness
Abuse of an Informal Carer
Mental health
Eating disorders
Discrimination
Bullying
Addiction
Body dysmorphia

Blood
& Love

For Marples

I want you to know
That I'm thinking of you
For whatever it is
That you're going through

You don't need to tell me
Your thoughts are your own
But I'm here if you need me
At the end of the phone

We can talk about anything
Other than this
We can laugh, we can cry
Give the subject a miss

But if you need to offload
I can do that too
I'm surprisingly resourceful
Just like you

Activist

What creates an activist?
An image
A lesson
A perspective shift?

What makes us speak up for others?
Our conscience
Their suffering
The pain of a mother?

How do we come to see
Beyond ourselves
Our wants
Our needs?

How do we learn to educate
Without accusation, blame and hate?

Why doesn't change happen fast
enough?
Now we know what we know
It's all too much

Now these images burn my eyes
The torture
No reason
Undisguised

How did we buy into this myth of
'dairy'
Of fields and families and animals
carefree

Why as children were we not told?
Of the abuse
Insemination
And babies stole

I wish I'd known sooner
But all I can do
Is inform myself and appeal to you
Share facts and not fiction
Let everyone see
The injustice
The abuse
The cruelty

In Your Eyes

Your aqua eyes radiate light
As if a torch shone from behind
Inspiration, ideas, love and care
Circle and bubble and blaze in there

A mind as sharp as a steel trap
A heart as wide as an open lake
For those who impose on your
beautiful nature
Will be their greatest of mistakes

Rich in history
Full of life lessons
Wise and kind
Grown beyond recognition

A loyal friend
A moral partner
Once entwined
Yours thereafter

What have I done to deserve this
treasure?
The joy and stimulation
The love and the pleasure

A gift of laughter
Of stretching my mind
Exhausting, exhilarating
A precious find

He is mine and I am his
Mirroring, but learning
A life more discerning

The Girl With The Red Hair

The girl with the red hair is kind and
sweet
The gentlest you could ever meet
Insightful, curious, wilful and brave
A sixth sense, a psychic; and true to
her name

Pure as snow; light as blossom
Pretty with big eyes and a powerful
bottom

A dancer; so graceful in form and in
nature
Her walk swings in time
Such a beautiful creature

One of a kind
Strong and protective
The sharpest of minds
She must be respected

Never again could there ever be
An entity so powerful as she

Life changing to meet
To be touched by her presence
A gift to receive
Just a dust of her essence

Claire

I almost forget
When I pick up the phone
To tell you a story
A small anecdote
That you are not there
And not coming back
Taken abruptly
An asthma attack

You were the first person
I called my best friend
I found that too cheesy
Something other girls did

But you weren't really like them
You were brutally real
So true and so funny
That was your appeal

Your hair in a knot
And brightly coloured jeans
Muddy DMs and wellies
Food on your sleeve

But such a beautiful person
Outside and in
Clever and vibrant
Tan olive skin

I remember your sister
She was so much like you
Asked me a question
To see if I knew

You were so young
She needed to know
If you had lived
And hit milestones

I reassured her
Or I hope that I did
That you milked every minute
Took the very best of it

Your life was too short
But I always knew
You made a mark on me
An imprint of you

Clara

There once was a girl
Of Irish descent
Who was young and courageous
On adventures she went

To meet other cultures
And from each visit find
What drives us and joins us
What makes humankind

She had big ambitions
To learn of life below sea
And make conservation
Her priority

She had much integrity
Morals and grace
A sharp active mind
And a beautiful face

She worked all hours
To follow her goals
Spent nights in the library
Took on many roles

Fiercely independent
Yet able to see
She was changing and growing
With her college family

All The Players; All The Daggers

You take my blood
Until I have none
I'm exhausted
I'm done

I'm half the person
I used to be
I'm tired, depleted
Just want to be me

When I let go; it was such a relief
A weight off my shoulders
So much lighter
Released

I could feel; almost immediate
My energy return
I could breathe a full breath
My chest didn't burn

I don't want to hear
All about you
It's repetitive; I'm bored
Do what you want to

I'm not a mother
So don't push me to be yours
Take responsibility, accountability
Be an adult; do chores

It's not my fault
You feel so bad about yourself
Don't turn that on me
I've tried everything to help

It's your job to seek guidance
For yourself; mend the cracks
You've worn me down now
And there's no going back

It is sad, sometimes shocking; when
things come to an end
We once were together; now barely a
friend
I'm angry; but I know in my gut this
will pass
You let me down; very badly
Some things aren't built to last

I am sorry, myself
For the things I did wrong
I tried my hardest; not enough
I became overwhelmed

But I learned from mistakes
Like we always do
I'll do better; be more aware from the
outset
And so will you too

It seems so crazy
That people never see
When on the inside; in the midst
How good it could be

Fail to appreciate
What we saw; at the very start
Take for granted and damage
A wide open heart

Life pushed us and knocked us
We tried to get up
But it was too much; a bombardment
So we turned it on us

What once was amusing
Became sore; always grating
Ever present; annoying
Eye rolling; irritating

At this point, it was clear
The damage was layers
Too ingrained, too deep
Too drained the players

So we strip off the shirts
Throw them down on the floor
And we stretch and rest
Tend our bruises and sores

For in time, we both know
We'll get back in the game
With a new perspective
With knowledge; and never the same

Befall

Why does misfortune befall
The nicest people of them all
Who give their energy freely
Who are selfless and not greedy

Why is it left to fate
Those taken early to heaven's gate
Who still have so much left to offer
When others do not wish to bother

Why are those who show the greatest
kindness
And lust for life
And love and brightness

Stolen from us
Made to suffer
Missed by loved ones
Why another?

Rose tinted spectacles

Why did I fail to see
The person right in front of me
Why did I ignore
When you show me who you are

Narcissist

I want to tell you a story about a girl
She had the world at her feet
That was before she was to meet
A narcissist

She was cool, cold as ice
She was fly, she had spice
Knew her own mind

She had dreams; he would take
She had confidence; he would shake
Made her doubt her own mind

Stamped on her boundaries
Laid hands on her skin
Turned her world outside in

Broke down her self-worth
Talked trash about her
Turned family against her
Made everyone doubt her

But from this place of being broken
down
Unbelievably, she reclaimed her
crown
With the help of her real friends
Her mother, her counsellor

From this place of despair
She proved herself able
To reclaim her life
Her seat at the table

Of her own path; her future, her joy
That she had somehow lost
For the sake of a boy

So what had she learned from these
years and this trauma
What lessons to relay to her nieces and
daughter

That respect for yourself; your wants
and your needs
Is paramount to nurturing the seed

Of your soul and its growth
That you must feed to flourish
It must be protected, heard and
respected

Now she can look in the mirror and
genuinely see
The beautiful girl she has always been

Free of his criticisms, taunts and jibes
Free of her tear filled red-rimmed eyes

Able to see him clear as day
A loser, a waster, full of venom and
spite
Trying to fill his own veins by
bleeding her dry

So she uses these lessons to educate
To give others strength to overcome
hate

To put the narcissists where they
belong
In the past, in the distance; in a life
long gone

You Bet

You bet, they die
Is their life
just 'a good time'
A chance to buy a hat
Drink lots of wine

Is it so important to you
To take photos with friends
Over their last breath
Through injury
A broken leg equals Death

Do you really think it's 'fun'
To have them drugged
Made to run

Why does your pleasure
Have more value
Than their whole being
Their life cut short

Have you ever thought
Of this 'industry'
Like any other
To make money
Animals suffer

Have you looked behind the lies
Of due care
Look at their eyes

Here you will see their pain
Truth untold
A reflection of your actions
Selfish and cold

The Carer

Who is the old man
Who sits in a chair
Wagging his finger
Talking worry; despair

Why does he torture
Belittle and poke
The people who help him
Care for him the most

What happened to the person
That he used to be
Jovial and courteous
Traits now unseen

Why now contrary
Awkward and rude
Full of anxiety
Hatred, abuse

It's not hard to imagine
How it must feel
To lose independence
Good health and zeal

But should I be punished
For his aging; for nature
Given never a thank you
For my efforts, my labour

I long for five minutes
A moment of peace
To gather my thoughts
To sit or to read

To look out the window
Without questions or chatter
Listen to the birds
Think of nothing that matters

Where has the man gone
Who was kind; who was funny
Now laughs at misfortune
Obsessed with his money

Is this a cruel trick
Of life and old age
That I grieve him during his lifetime
Instead of in the grave

Investigators

Thank you for doing
What I never could
Confronting the abuse
The pain and the blood

Shining a light
On the darkest of places
Brutality, torture
Cruel confined spaces

Thank you for witnessing
With your own eyes
Their pain, their suffering
Their screams, their cries

For bringing out in the open
For the world to see
The barbarism
Of this 'industry'

The culling, grinding, gassing and
cages
Enslavement, entrapment and 'rotary
milking'

How has it been hidden
Disguised and misnamed
This deeply disturbing
Human shame

Thank you for making us aware
Of reality
No excuses
All laid bare

Thank you for hurting
Your own hearts
To make change
To change minds
Despite the scars

Conditioning

Old habits die hard
This I know to be true
That's why I'm torturing myself
Instead of challenging you

Finding fault in myself
Picking my arguments carefully
Accepting little jibes
Instead of meeting them squarely

It's why I cry in the toilet
In public spaces
Instead of taking my leave
Despite all consequences

It's why I put my needs
Below everyone else
To the point I'm so tired
I have nothing left

But I'm assertive and strong
And I expect a lot
Yet I'm a woman; so I'm told
Be grateful for what you've got

Someone faithful and kind
Who loves you is a gift
Doesn't matter if they take
More than they give

But I'm trying to undo
All that I've been told
I'm entitled to be angry
Rash or bold

These characteristics are not exclusive
to you
So I'll do what I want now
To myself I'll be true

Black Cat

I went to see a psychic
And she told me that I'd see
The image of a black cat
So I'd know you're here with me

So if I'm feeling wary
Uncertain or alone
I look outside my window
For a black cat running home

Their leaps from out the shadows
Their graceful prowl and strength
Reminds me of your courage
Your wisdom and presence

I wonder at their beauty
Their eyes so sharp and bright
I take comfort that you're near me
As they vanish into night

Spoils

How must it feel
To watch the wild run free
On their land; in their space
Without captivity

How must it feel
To hear a stampede thunder
To feel the cracked warm earth
To watch a burning sunset

What possesses man
To want to soil
The beauty of nature
With his hunting spoils

What does it say
About a creature
That kills for pleasure
A repellent reaper

Yet

I knew, you knew, yet...
It remained unspoken still
'til death, I regret

Fear &
Rage

Every Hour

You spiked my drink
More than once
Invaded my body
Abused my trust

You didn't care
About a consequence
Just you own plan
And executing it

I don't like to think
Of what might have been
If I hadn't shocked you
Taken my leave

That was bad enough
But I brush it off
Like many do
It affects all of us

I often think
Of my 'lucky escapes'
Three in number
What a disgrace

But don't pity me
I am always aware
That far worse exists
So gross, so unfair

So much abuse
The imbalance of power
No justice for victims
Six women killed every hour

She

She walked to the water
And stood at the edge
Behind the railing
But up on the ledge

She opened her mouth
Screamed as hard as she could
I hate you, I hate you
It made her feel good

Before this it burned her
She needed release
The angry disappointment
She couldn't find peace

So she shoved it
And pushed it
Right out of her mouth
The fear and the hatred
Her feelings burst out

Hot tears filled her eyes
And rushed down her face
Why do I deserve
To be in this place

What have I done?
I need to know please?
To receive without willing
This grisly disease

How do I fix this?
Where do I start?
I don't understand it?
It's broken my heart

The wind pushed her forward
Blew her hair in her face
The waves hit the bricks
Threw up salt she could taste

The wildness calmed her
Gave her clarity to see
She was strong
She could fight this
She would beat this disease

Revenge

This is a story about revenge
Is it the place where bitterness ends?

A place for angry feelings to go
A chance to act out
Lash out
Spread woe

Action can be as healthy as tears
A focus
Distraction
Avoiding our fears

But what I've learned
Now easy to see
The greatest revenge is none
Because you have no hold on me

Anxiety

What does it feel like in your chest?
Contraction
Distraction
Breathlessness

What does it feel like in your mind?
Thoughts running
Invading
Override

What does it feel like in your gut?
Sickness
Discomfort
Unease, reflux

How do we make it go away?
Breathe deeply
Sit quietly
Assess forces at play

Mark time as your own
Make your boundaries clear
This way we help anxiety disappear

The Ballerina

The ballerina
Dances life
Light as air
No stress, no strife

Gliding, smiling
Without a care
Not flustered; harassed
No worry, no wear

Yet beneath her smile
At closer view
Is much pain
And anger too

Rage repressed
And dreams abandoned
Bad decisions
World unexpanded

Safe
In her familiar bubble
Yet uninspired
No risk; no trouble

What is life
If not lived
To its extent
With pain and vim

Chances taken
Bonds get broken
Image reformed
And thoughts outspoken

All the mess
Is all the glory
Learning, yearning
That's the story

Tests of character
Essence, morals
You may break
But then you'll blossom

Losing control might be the key
To unlock what lies beneath

Why?

Why do you insist I be
Something that I cannot see
A person I can't recognise
My face
My place
My role
My eyes

Why do you want me to perform;
To societal stereotypes and norms
To hit milestones of age and gain
When it's evident this causes pain

Why do you want me to behave
Appropriately, quietly; and well
trained
Why can't I let my talents show
My spirit
Sparkle
Humour
Glow

Why should I keep my self shrouded
Identity disguised and feelings
clouded
Why can't you just let it be
You be you
And I'll be me

Sweetheart

It's not your problem sweetheart
What I choose to do
With my hard earned cash
Who I give it to

It's not your problem sweetheart
If you cannot see
That you are devoid
Of empathy

It's not my problem sweetheart
That your upturned nose
Has inspired
My critical prose

The judgement
The scathing on your face
Show you up
You're a disgrace

Her Tongue Was A Weapon

She tried on many hats
From the day she reached her teens
From Earth Mother to rock groupie
And all things in between

She liked to get attention
Never cared if good or bad
The chaos and the violence
Belied the childhood she'd had

She damaged all who touched her
Turned their lives to fire and ash
She danced amongst the flames
Fed on every row and clash

Her actions confounded experts
As they floundered to explain
What was her motivation
Had she suffered untold pain

Her tongue was a weapon
She enjoyed the aftermath
As she aged it was clear
She was a psychopath

The Stamp Collector

The Stamp Collector
Finds treasure in trash
Uses stamps to replace
The things he never had

Finds value in faults
Displays his precious finds with care
His collection surrounds him
He finds comfort there

Some stamps like old friends
They've been here a long while
Ever-present; never changing
The memories make him smile

Some are from distant places
That he will never see
But he likes to imagine
Them travelling overseas

Every stamp brought a message
From one person to another
But the stamp collector looks
For only stamps to discover

People let him down
He lost bonds along the way
But when he bids his stamps
goodnight
He knows they're here to stay

Merry-Go-Round

Why so frustrating
The simplest of tasks
A payment
A purchase
A question to ask

Why all the waiting
The music ear worms
The jangling
Repetition
When is my turn?

Why greeted abruptly
No will to assist
Evasive
Impatient
Just ticked off a list

I know it is money
That makes it this way
Go faster
Work harder
Reduce worker pay
Push substandard products
Give inadequate care
Block all efforts at contact
The profit lies there

So why do we choose this
Allow this, lie down
Because we are exhausted
By this merry-go-round

Hey

Hey man
It's not for you to see
And comment on
My disability

Hey man
It's not for you to know
Why I limp
Or walk 'too slow'

Hey man
It's not for me to explain
This brace on my leg
My diagnosis name

Hey man
Just let me be
No need for you to judge
Understand or agree

Hey man
How would you like
To receive opinions
Intrusion in your life

Hey man
How would you like to discuss
Your most personal failings
Because there's no trust

Hey man
How would you feel to be told
That you are a problem
For being ill, being old

Hey man
Would you not rather see
That there is care; is help
In case you become me

What Happened To You?

From total control
To loss of control
What happened to you?

I would hope
To understand
What you're going through

I would like to help
If I can
Offer an ear

I want to burst
The morning smog
Make the pain disappear

That frantic movement
With little fuel
Seemed punishingly cruel

But it's what you knew
What you did
They were your 'rules'

But now I see
Something worse
Pain in your eyes

You don't want to be
Here with us
However you try

So now you flip
Another sip
From nothing to all

Spend your day
In a stupor
Little recall

What it is
That broke your heart
Made you want

To block it out
Take it down
Just give up

Karma

You're ugly on the outside
As you are in
Spite drips off your tongue
Green tones in your skin

I can't help but hear you
As I sit on this train
Laugh at others misfortune
Their fear and their pain

I don't find it funny
As you snort down your nose
Mock a disabled puppy
You're the epitome of gross

You're waving your finger
Clearly trying to claim
For the wrong reasons
The attention you crave

Your chorus of hyenas
As rancid as you
Now targeting a child
That all of you knew

Saying you'll send him
'Just for a laugh'
'Jokes' about his deafness
Where are your hearts?

I don't understand it
What caused you to be
So bitter, so stupid
So careless; all three

But karma is a storm
When visited upon you
Perhaps you'll receive
What you are due

How Much?

How much time do we spend
Waiting for the week days end
Waiting for our cheque to come
Waiting 'til we can go home

How much energy do we waste
Wishing away a mistake
Regretting things we have said
Lying sleepless in our beds

How many times do we accept
Treatment we should not expect
Statements deliberately unkind
Those who give us no respect

What does it take
To make us think
Draw the line
Make the link

Our time is dear
Our energy precious
Don't waste it on drains
Only radiators

Gratitude

Not Wholesome Content   Samantha EJ Button

Perfectly Perfect

Perfectly, perfect
That belongs to you
Precious and kind
Despite all you go through

Clever and observant
Thoughtful and sweet
Specific and unswerving
A treasure complete

Deliciously, delicious
Bright eyed; full of fire
Curiosity and passion
Everything I desire

Face Off

Why put on that face
What's so wrong
With the one
That lies beneath

Why mis-shape your eyes
Mouth, nose; or cheekbones
Why the dislike
Of those you own

Why do we feel the need
To live our lives
So publicly
Full of fallacies

Why is our self-esteem
Reliant on others regard
A compliment-dependency

Who sets these rules
To be this way or that
Too slim, too fat
Satisfaction-impossibility

Is it all to distract
From being alert
Questioning what's right
Engaging in life

Wouldn't it be wild
To appreciate
Our mistakes
And what makes us unique

Why is that a fringe belief
Not the 'norm'
Anti-establishment
What a travesty

Just for one moment
Take the chance
To recognise
Who you are

Behind the mask
Who exists
What you have
Still to give

What a difference
You could make
Living by your own rules
Making waves

I Have Time To Learn

Time to learn
I have the good fortune
To be gifted these years
Birthright, location

To have a window
Within my responsibilities
To take time to read
To listen, take opportunities

So I shall not waste this
I will always enquire
Keep my mind open
Beyond my desires

Beyond my own experiences
My own pain
My own place
For what I have learned
Is I am but a small piece

Shotguns

I heard talking in the forest
Shotguns echo in the air
In a place unfamiliar
The three of us were there

We had suffered many setbacks
Obstacles to work through
But I knew then, as always
I'd risk my life for you two

I felt pain at your discomfort
Helplessness at your despair
But we armed ourselves with iron
Faced our fears front and square

And of course we overcame
All that was thrown in our paths
But it was not without a tear shed
And a scar on our hearts

But in all of this a lesson
Something good from the bad
That we three were resilient
A stronger love could not be found

Review

A moment alone with my thoughts
No noise, no screen, no ones and
noughts
No influence; no conversation
Just flight and colour and inspiration

Waves of cloud across the sky
Still and luminous as sun sets
Bird settling down and wildlife rising
Trees and shrubs in silhouette

What are the things I need to do?
I push the list, with force, away
Revel instead in memories
Unburdened, unfiltered, a meze of
days

Allow myself a brief reflection
What do I need more of?
Need less of?
Casual introspection

Am I where
I expected to be?
Does that matter; I'm alive
I have much, I am free

As we grew
We had hope; expectations
Lines in the sand
Unexpected complications

But if we are lucky
These were smashed and reformed
For that is where
Our growth is born

As I think of advice
Given freely by elders
'Value love above all'
'Appreciate your parents'

'Don't get hung up on material things'
'Just enough; is enough'
'Value life; all it brings'

I believe overall
My decisions were good
I was brave, kept my values
Treated others as I should
I gained little of significance;
in monetary worth
Yet achieved much
In experiences, learning and love

Nina

Nina
Made me laugh
From the first time
I cast eyes
On her site

Nina
Gave me confidence
To be proud
Of the changes
In my life

Nina
Made me question
Why others intrude
On my privacy

Nina
Made me rethink
And appreciate
What it means
To be me

Nina
Changed my perspective
On what I found
As much as lost

Nina
Had to tell you
You gave hope
When I was lost

Nina
You're a diamond
brave mouth; big heart
Full of truth and positivity

Thank you
For all you've done
For our disabled community

Shiny Floor

I loved the house with the shiny floor
The big window and the bright red
door
It didn't take a lot of care
I have many happy memories there

We watched the foxes play at night
Our table held by cable ties
A home of love and energy
The 'get to know' of you and me

A moment of only simple pleasures
Us four, together, finding treasures
Exploring, absorbing, hope abounds
A foundation built; strong and sound

Box Of Treasure

A little box of treasure
Sits perched above the arch
In it many secrets
And stories made 'to art

A thoughtful stem of flower
A swish of blended paint
Tales of joy and laughter
Anger, rage and hate

Anxiety sewn through stitches
Despair layered light in card
Love stirred and set in resin
Pain carved into a heart

All of these creations
Much more than what they seem
This little box of treasures
So dear to you and me

Gratitude

He walked a little further
To escape the crowd
Sat on a bench
As the rain came down

He cherished the sights
Trees reflected in the lake
Stone walls over fields
Ate the sandwich she'd made

Some ducks waddled over
Fought over the crust
He breathed in the damp air
The leaves smelt of musk

He thought of how fortunate
He was to be
Sat in the stillness
Amongst all the trees

Overlooking the water
Still clean, cold and clear
Remembering people
He held ever dear

How grateful he was
To have time to himself
To daydream and ponder
To be in good health

He thought of the people
He treasured the most
Small in their number
And always kept close

Many things of beauty
He had felt and seen
Love, adventure and travel
And all things between

From his demeanour
You could never have known
His struggles and childhood
His battles overcome

Just another silver fox
A wry smile on his face
Don't judge a book by its cover
For you'll make a mistake

The Lady in the Post Office

The lady at the post office forgot to say
please
Was rude and abrupt
Loud with urgency

Thought herself above her 'server'
Pushed herself forward
With some fervour

I try think what made her be
Devoid of manners and elegancy
Illness, bereavement, money trouble?
An insular consuming worry bubble

When confronted with rudeness; I try
to think
What's making their behaviour stink?
What are the struggles and misfortune
Causing frowning and distortion?

I try to have some empathy
Beyond the surface I can see
I try to give some wiggle room
They're not themselves; let's assume

But more than this
What's most important
Is making sure
We're not absorbent

To not claim
Consume or take
Negative energy we can't shake

If we keep our own manners
Treat others with care
Be courteous and grateful
There's happiness there

When we put out effort;
Into the world
We make something brighter
Fearless and bold

Say It Now

Say it now
Just in case
You never see
Another day break

Do it now
Just sit and start
Your opinion matters
Your thoughts, your art

Speak it now
Loud and fierce
It matters to you
You're an activist

Choose it now
How you spend your time
Who you give your presence
Do your values align?

Make it now
The change you want to begin
Step forward, not backward
Let new energy in

The Queue

One problem at a time
That's all you can do
Let them form an orderly line
Work your way through

Try just to focus
One hour of each day
To scratch a problem off the list
Or merely chip away

You cannot help others
From an empty chest
You must protect your sanity
Mark time out to rest

As much as you are obligated
Relied upon too
There is but one who needs you most
That person is you

Those Who Know, Know

My hands don't work as well as they
should
And I'm desperately tired
And my balance isn't good

But there's a lot of activity in my brain
Lots of sparks and false starts
But some good all the same

And I can't do the things that I used to
do
So I cried and I grieved
For those losses too soon

But I do have a will to do something
more
But it might be outside
An 'incapacity' score

That makes it no less worth being
shown
It's a message, it matters
And those who know, know

Printed in Great Britain
by Amazon